Black History in the Americas

By Arthur H Tafero

Forward

The history of people of color in the Americas is both inspirational and tragic. The accomplishments of blacks in the Americas is undeniable, and the extent of their suffering before achieving many of their accolades is seldom explored in detail. This book takes an overview look at the history of the evolution of the black experience in the Americas.

We trace the first victims of the European slave trade (in conjunction with the Arab slave trade) to their unfortunate placement in the Caribbean Islands in the very late 15th century under the flag of Queen Isabella and King Ferdinand of Spain and follow the plight of the slave trade for the next three hundred and fifty years.

Three hundred and fifty years is a long time to be under the wheel of injustice, but the fortunes of transplanted blacks did not end after the Civil War in 1865. There was still another hundred and forty years of discrimination and poverty in store for the descendents of the former slaves in every part of the Western Hemisphere.

These lesson plan outlines trace the battles of the Reconstruction Era, the flight of blacks to the cities of Northeast America, and the eventual victory of the Civil Rights movement begun in the early 1960s. With the election of the first black president of the United States in 2008 with Barack Obama, the efforts of blacks to assert themselves in America finally reached its pinnacle.

With outstanding accomplishments in science, technology, baseball, movies, basketball, literature, football, art, dance, and business, Black Americans and blacks in the rest of the Americas have emerged with great dignity and pride. This book is just a small sample of their accomplishments.

Course Description – Black History in the Americas is an overview of the Black Experience from the time of the first Portuguese colonies in Africa until the beginning of the 21st Century. Topics will include, but not be limited to: The African Slave Trade, Early Free Blacks in America, Slavery in the Western Hemisphere, Slavery and the Cotton Industry in the South, The Reconstruction Period, Black Family Dispersion, Slave Migrations, Blacks in the Caribbean, Black Migrations Within America, Blacks in American Cities, Blacks and Stereotyping, Black Political History, Black Economic History, Black Religious History, Blacks in the 21st Century in the Americas, Blacks in Sports, Black Educational Leaders and Notable Black Contributions.

Primary Text: *Roots* – Alex Haley
Secondary Texts: *The Souls of Black Folk* - W.E.B. Dubois
Caribbean Slave Society and Economy – Beckles & Sheperd

Lesson 1 – Africa and the Slave Trade in the Fifteenth Century

Handouts

Map of 15th Century Africa
Map of 15th Century Caribbean
Map of 15th Century South America

Content

A. The first country to establish the slave trade in Africa was Portugal in the early 15th century.

B. Portugal originally established colonies in Africa in the early 15th century; enslaving local populations as they expanded their control.

C. Portugal first colonized parts of the Caribbean and Brazil and enslaved their local inhabitants by the 16th Century. They were able to do this because of Prince Henry the Navigator and his superior map-making ability.

D. After expanding their territories in the Caribbean and Brazil, Portugal come to the conclusion that it needed more manpower as slaves in these new Western Hemisphere areas.

E. The conclusion was to ship additional slaves from Africa to the Caribbean and Brazil.

F. Following Brazil, Spain and other European nations began to expand into colonies in Africa and the Western Hemisphere by the beginning of the 16th Century.

G. As expansion into the Western Hemishphere developed, slavery in both Africa and the new developing territories in the Western Hemisphere increased proportionately.

Critical Questions:

1. Why do you think Portugal expanded its territories to Africa and the Western Hemisphere?

2. How was Portugal able to make these expansions when richer and more powerful nations were not?

3. Why did the Portuguese begin shipping slaves from Africa to the Western Hemisphere?

4. How did the Portuguese establish a ready-made supply of slaves in Africa for Shipment to the Western Hemisphere?

5. Why did the other European nations follow Portugal into Africa?

6. Why did the other European nations follow Spain and Portugal into the Western Hemisphere?

7. How did the expansion of these European nations into Africa and the Western Hemisphere affect the Slave Trade?

Additional Internet Resources for this Lesson:
www.pbs.org/wgbh/aia/part1/1narr3.html
www.cocc.edu/cagatucci/classes/hum211/timelines/htimeline3.htm
http://www.thinkquest.org/library/site_sum.html?tname=13406&url=13406/ta/2.htm

LESSON 2 – Free Blacks in the Americas

Handouts

Photos of Free Blacks in North America
Photos of Free Blacks in South America and Caribbean

Content

A. Free blacks first appeared in roughly the same order of
   territories that encountered black slavery in the South
   American and Caribbean regions.

B. The first free blacks in the South American and Caribbean
   areas were former slaves that had been freed by their
   masters for a variety of reasons; the most common reason
   was the death of the master and wills that provided for the
   release of a slave or slaves.

C. As slavery moved slowly through the Caribbean and South

America, more and more slaves were freed.

D. Some freed slaves attempted to gain passage back to Africa, but the vast majority tried to make the best of it where they were located.

E. Gradually, slaves in North America also began to gain small numbers of freed men. First starting in the South and then continuing into the North.

F. Despite these developments, the vast majority of blacks in both North and South America were slaves rather than free men.

G. In certain instances, free blacks were once again made slaves for various reasons including not having papers proving they had been freed and kidnapping by slave owners from other areas.

H. Free blacks in all areas were not considered equals to whites economically, politically and socially.

Critical Questions

1. Why did free blacks first appear in the South American and Caribbean regions?

2. How was it possible that slaves became to be free before general emancipation?
3. Why was there an inevitable increase in freed slaves over time?

4. What were the options of slaves once they became free?

5. Why were North American slaves the last to benefit the gift of freedom from their former owners?

6. Why was it that the vast majority of blacks in both Americas still remained slaves?

7. How were some of these former slaves and free men made into slaves once again?

8. Why, despite papers stating they were free, were blacks still considered economically, politically and socially unequal?

Additional Internet Resources for this Lesson:

www.kidinfo.com/American_History/Colonization_Colonial_Life.html
www.blacksandjews.com/Schorsch.html
ipoaa.com/blacks_latin_america_etc.html
saxakali.com/caribbean/shamil.html

LESSON 3 – The Early Slave Trade in the Americas

handouts:

Art of early slave trade in Africa
Art of early slave trade in the Americas

Content

A. Portugal was quickly followed by Spain in the activity of first creating colonies, then slave markets in Africa. These two countries were the primary European traders in this market.

B. Because of the Columbus expeditions, Spain was to overtake Portugal in

in territories in the Western Hemisphere. The slave trade quickly followed in any area the Spanish settled.

C. While Portugal still maintained an important presence in Brazil, Spain Now was dominant in the Caribbean and in Florida.

D. Saint Augustine, Florida was the center of the slave trade in the early part of the 16th century, shortly after Columbus was in the Caribbean.

E. Early settlements in the northern part of North America were relatively devoid of African slaves as the early New England settlements depended mostly on indentured servants for menial labor.

E. The cultivation of tobacco and cotton were to change the nature of many of the working requirements of the early colonies.

F. The primary source for labor in these new markets (Tobacco and cotton) were to become slaves rather than indentured servants.

G. Increased demand for the new products of tobacco and cotton also increased the demand for slaves. This induced other countries other than Portugal and Spain to become involved in the slave trade.

H. England and various colonies within North America became involved in the slave trade in order to compete economically with European powers.

Critical Questions

1. Why did Spain quickly follow Portugal in Africa and the Western Hemisphere?

2. What advantage did Spain have over Portugal in the Western Hemisphere?

3. How did Spain become dominant in the Caribbean and Florida?

4. Why was the slave trade center at Saint Augustine, Florida an important development for slavery in North America?

5. Why were settlements in the northern part of the colonies relatively slave-free?

6. How did the new crops of tobacco and cotton affect the workforce of the colonies?

7. How did Portugal and Spain's success in the slave trade affect other

European powers and the colonies?

Additional Internet Resources for this Lesson

www.africana.com/research/encarta/trading.asp
www.africasia.com/newafrican/may00/nacs0502.htm
library.thinkquest.org/13406/ta/2.htm

LESSON 4 - The Slave Trade and Cotton Industry in the Southern Colonies

Handouts:
Map of the southern colonies
Art of plantation slavery

Content

A. Eventually, cotton dwarfed the production of tobacco in the southern colonies. As a labor-intensive industry, cotton required the introduction of more slaves into the southern colonies.

B. Most of the early slaves in the southern colonies were imported from the Caribbean; usually stopping at Saint Augustine in Florida.

C. The slave trade in the southern colonies evolved with the direct transport of slaves either from the Caribbean or Africa itself. The stop at Saint Augustine was gradually reduced.

D. A number of the southern colonies now could finance the complete cycle of the slave trade from capturing slaves in Africa to transporting them directly to ports within the southern colonies.

E. Treatment of the slaves varied from cruel to well-cared for as slaves were considered to be economic assets and investments which required professional maintenance.

F. The emotional and physical toll on blacks captured to become slaves in both the Caribbean and the colonies was incalculable. The effects of the slave trade still resound our communities well into the present day.

G. The slave trade was an important foundation for the development of racism within the United States. The freeing of the slaves (The Emancipation Proclamation) did little to eliminate over three hundred years of racism reinforced by the slave trade.

H. The southern colonies had now become almost totally dependent on the slave trade as a major economic component of industry in the South.

Critical Questions

1. Why did the southern colonies need more slaves as the cotton industry increased in the region?

2. How did the origins of the slaves used in the southern colonies evolve as the economies of the southern colonies evolved?

3. Why was a change of the origin of slaves used in the southern colonies important?

4. Why did some slaveowners treat their slaves well, while others mistreated their slaves?

5. What were some of the emotional and physical tolls of slavery?

6. Why would slavery be a natural breeding ground for racism?

7. How did the southern colonies become dependent on slavery?

8. How did the dependency on slavery force the South into war with the North?

Additional Internet Resources for this Lesson:
www.pbs.org/wgbh/aia/part3/3narr6.html
www.civilwarhome.com/kingcotton.htm
www.beyondbooks.org/slavery/slaverygrowth.htm

LESSON 5 – The Effects of the Reconstruction Period

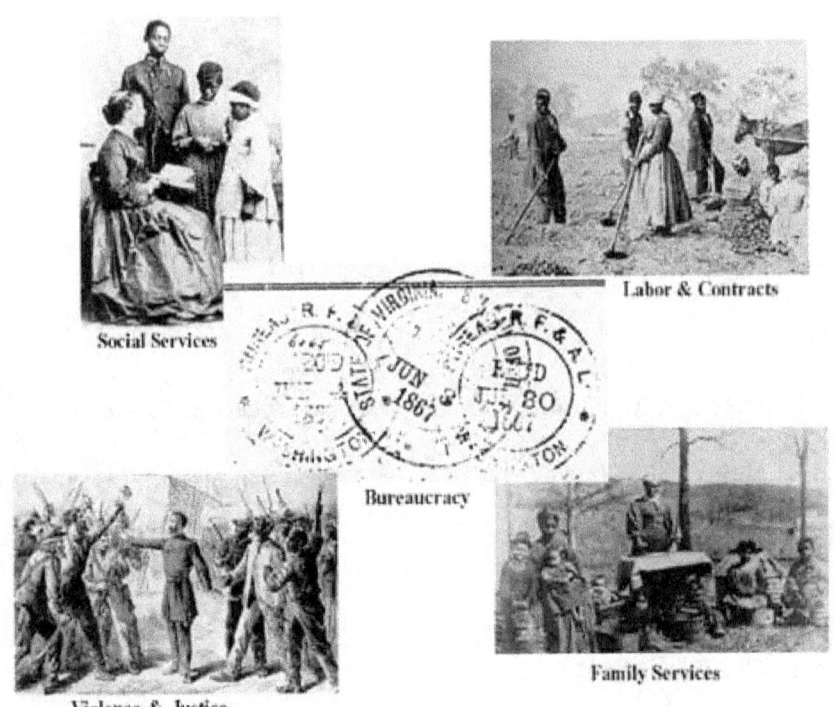

Social Services

Labor & Contracts

Bureaucracy

Violence & Justice

Family Services

Handouts
Map of the US after the Civil War
Photos of Reconstruction

Content

    A. After the Civil War, the effects of slavery continued to beset black families.

    B. Black families had gone through at least three separations once captured by slave traders: the horrific initial separation from their tribes in their original kidnapping, family separations at the primary slave-selling areas such as Saint Augustine, Florida, and additional separations at the whim of the slave-owners who could sell off children or brothers and sisters at will.

    C. As of a result of these oppressive practices, black families had to overcome almost impossible odds in order to maintain family ties and normal family interaction.

D. Family dispersions as a result of these experiences negatively impacted black families well into the 20th century. Some sociologists have suggested That the effect continues into the 21st century for some families.

E. Although blacks had supposed equality in the South after the Civil War, the Southern white infrastructure was not ready to accept them into the mainstream of Southern society.

F. The Ku Klux Klan was both a reaction to Northern excesses in legislation which disenfranchised whites for the first time and to blacks, who whites felt were taking a portion of their political and economic power away from them.

G. Reaction of blacks during the Reconstruction Period varied from staying on as paid free men on some plantations, to cultivating the forty acres they had given by the US government on their own. Many blacks, who could not bear reminders of slavery, dispersed into the large cities of the South and some dispersed even further away into the North. Washington, DC was one of the Northern cities blacks would come into contact with.

H. Many blacks had extremely difficult transitions in both Southern and Northern cities as racism was about equally prevalent in both areas. *Jim Crow* laws, a set of repressive laws against blacks written by local Southern whites, became the norm in the South.

Critical Questions

1. Why did the effects of slavery continue to affect blacks after the Civil War?

2. Why was separation a constant threat to black families?

3. Why was maintaining a family during slavery an extremely difficult task?

4. Why do you think family dispersions would take place as a result of these experiences of black families?

5. Why did Southern whites refuse to accept blacks into Southern society after the Civil War?

6. Why was the Ku Klux Klan formed?

7. Why did some blacks stay in the South and others move to the North after the Civil War?

8. How did racism make things almost as difficult for blacks after slavery as life was during slavery?

Additional Internet Resources for this Lesson
lcweb2.loc.gov/ammem/aaohtml/exhibit/aopart5.html
www.rit.edu/~nrcgsh/bx/bx06b.html
www.pointsouth.com/csanet/kkk.htm

LESSON 6 – BLACK FAMILY DISPERSION

Handouts:

Maps of 15th-19th century Africa
Maps of 15th-19th century Caribbean
Maps of 15th-19th century Americas

Content

A. Shortly after Portuguese colonization, slave trade practices in the early 15th century began to impact on African families.

B. If even only one family member was captured, black family dispersion could easily take place. Loss of mothers, fathers, sons and daughters impacted black families immediately after abduction.

C. If an entire family was captured by slave traders, other unfortunate events could conspire to break them up. At the main gathering areas on the West Coast of Africa, these families were often broken up and sold to different ships transporting the slaves to the Western Hemisphere.

D. If, by a stroke of luck, one whole family was captured together and sold together to one ship (and this did not happen often), the family faced another likelihood of being broken up as soon as they landed on the Western Hemisphere port (such as Haiti or Saint Augustine). The odds a whole family would survive these occurrences (as well as the horrendous voyage) were quite slim.

E. Once sold to a slave owner, remnants of a family would often face further deterioration if the slave owner had more than one plantation, which was often the case.

F. At this point in time, a black family in 15th century Africa could have had an entire family dispersed from capture, dispersion at the West African slave depot, disease and death on the voyage, dispersion at the Western Hemisphere slave depot and dispersion by various slave owners.

G. Further black family dispersion occurred after the Civil War when family members sometimes migrated to the cities of the South or North.

Critical Questions

1. How did Portuguese colonization of parts of Africa affect African families?

2. Why were the odds heavily against a black family staying together as a slave family?

3. Why were the main slave trading depots in West Africa a great threat to African families staying together?

4. Why was the voyage of the slaves a great threat to the family unit?

5. How did slave depots in the Western Hemisphere impact on black families?

6. How did slave owners impact the continuity of black families?

7. How did the Reconstruction Period impact on the continuity of black families?

Additional Internet Resources for this Lesson:
www.vmfa.state.va.us/hyman/hyman_migration1.html
highbeam.com/library/doc0.asp?docid=1P1:28840003&refid=ink_puball mags
us.history.wisc.edu/hist102/lectures/lecture09.html

LESSON 7 – Slave Migrations

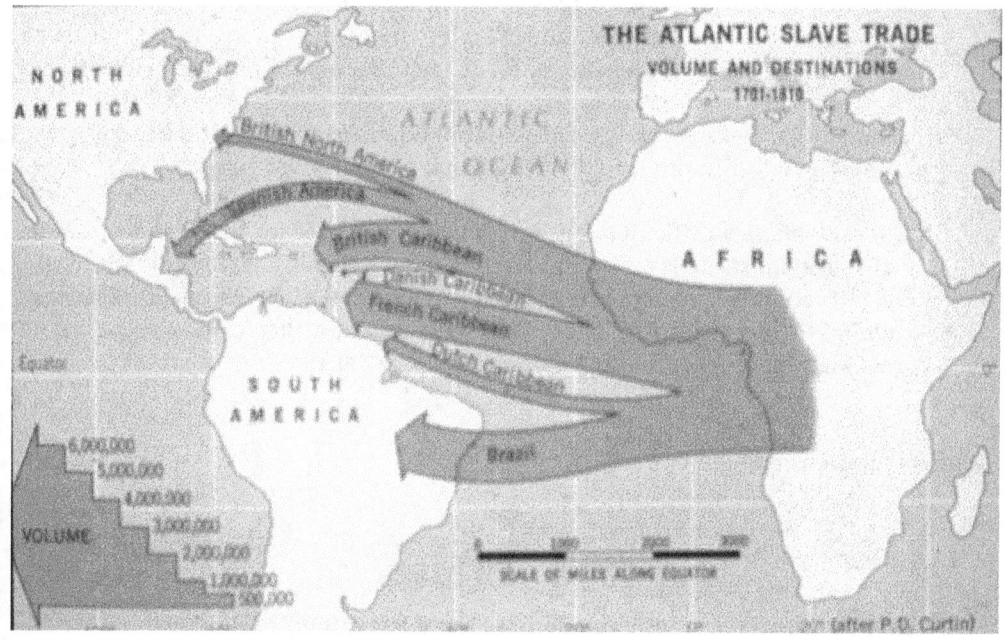

Handouts:
Maps of 15th-19th century Americas

Content

A. Initially, slave migrations started from whatever village in which they were captured to the primary slave trade depots on the West Coast of Africa. Some slaves were transported over a thousand miles to these depots.

B. Slaves further migrated as ships took them to the Western Hemisphere, including the Caribbean, South America and North America.

C. Once landing in the Caribbean, slave migrated to every corner of the islands, including Haiti, the Dominican Republic, Cuba, the Virgin Islands, the Bahamas and many others.

D. Some early slaves were left in Brazil and migrated to all parts of South America. Slaves generally worked in the coastal areas and plantations.

E. Slaves dropped off at Saint Augustine, Florida and points north migrated to every part of the colonies, but the vast majority of slaves were in the Southern colonies due to the needs of a work force for tobacco and particularly cotton.

F. Families of slaves generally went to many separate areas within the colonies and had a very difficult time keeping track of their loved ones.

G. Illiteracy made a difficult situation almost impossible for many slave families as it was against the law in many areas to teach slaves how to read and write. This forced illiteracy kept slaves from learning the whereabouts of relatives, learning the geography of where they were and how they could escape, and prevented them from making a decent living after the Civil War.

Critical Questions

1. How did the first slave migrations begin?

2. How did the slave ships contribute to slave migration?

3. How did slaves migrate through the Caribbean?

4. How did slaves migrate through South America?

5. How did slaves migrate through North America?

6. Once within a specific colony, how did slaves further disperse?

7. How did illiteracy affect the migration of slaves and how did it affect them after the Civil War?

Additional Internet Resources for this Lesson

scriptorium.lib.duke.edu/slavery/migration.html
fisher.lib.virginia.edu/collections/stats/slavetrade/mapmethod.html
www.vmfa.state.va.us/hyman/hyman_migration1.html

LESSON 8 - Slaves in the Caribbean

Handouts:
Maps of 15th-19th century Caribbean
Art and photos of Caribbean Slavery

Content

A. Slavery existed in both South America and the Caribbean prior to the European slave trade, however, the European slave trade was far more extensive.

B. Blacks brought to the Caribbean from Africa came to a climate that was similar to that of the one they left behind, but new diseases killed thousands as they arrived.

C. Eventually, the Spanish became dominant in the Caribbean. Slaves on each of the islands were treated differently. Some of the islands had harsh treatment of slaves and others treated their slaves fairly well and considered them investments.

D. Caribbean slaves were sometimes taken to either Saint Augustine or to the mainland of South America. There was no guarantee that they would be treated better where they were going.

E. Caribbean slaves had the same family dispersion problems that slaves in South America and North America had.

F. The social interaction of blacks with the general population in the Caribbean was less restrictive than that of life on the plantations in the Southern colonies.

G. Many slaves and ex-slaves in the Caribbean intermarried with the local populations in contrast to the slaves in the Southern colonies.

Critical Questions

1. How did pre-Columbian slavery compare to European slavery in the Caribbean?

2. How did climate and health conditions compare between Africa and the Caribbean?

3. How did treatment of slaves vary from the Caribbean to South and North America?

4. How did the dispersion problems of slaves in the Caribbean compare to to the slaves of North and South America?

5. How did the social interaction between slaves in the Caribbean and the general population differ from that of the slaves and the general population in the Southern colonies?

6. Why do you think the Spanish became dominant in the Caribbean?

7. Why were there many more marriages between the slaves of the Caribbean and the general populace than there were among the slaves of the Southern colonies and the general populace?

Additional Internet Resources for this Lesson
www.mrdowling.com/710-slavery.html
en.wikipedia.org/wiki/Slavery
books.cambridge.org/0521533201.html

LESSON 9 – Black Migrations Within North America

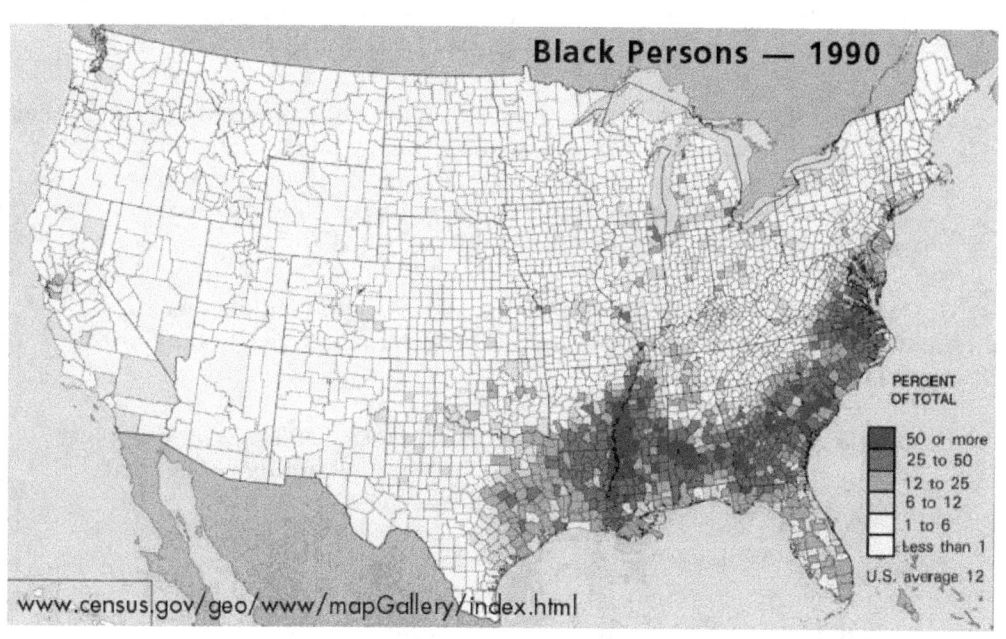

Black Persons — 1990

PERCENT OF TOTAL

50 or more
25 to 50
12 to 25
6 to 12
1 to 6
Less than 1

U.S. average 12

www.census.gov/geo/www/mapGallery/index.html

Handouts:
Maps of 16th to 20th century North America

Content

A. Initial migration of blacks in America began with the slave depot in Saint Augustine, Florida. Slaves from this depot usually were transported either by ship or horse north of Florida.

B. A few of the slaves from Africa and the Caribbean stayed in Saint Augustine, but the vast majority moved on to points north such as Georgia and South Carolina. Some even went as far as North Carolina and Virginia.

C. Later migrations included slave movements to the deep South such as Louisiana, Mississippi, Arkansas and points west and north.

D. After the Civil War, black migrations from the coastal cities usually proceeded north. A slave in Atlanta would often move to Washington, DC. Other northern destinations were often Philadelphia, Baltimore and New York.

E. As blacks streamed into the inner cities of these large urban areas, whites gradually moved to the outer areas of the cities, creating the large "suburbs". These white suburbs were primarily racist in nature until the latter half of the 20th century.

F. Occasionally, successful blacks would also move into these suburbs to escape the teeming new numbers of peoples now coming into the cities in addition to freed slaves. Social interaction was still limited, however, to rampant racism. This situation was exacerbated by the large increase in European immigration at the same time the Civil War ended.

G. Occasionally, blacks would sail back to Africa, but found life there too different from what they had grown used to. Most would return to the United States and try to begin anew.

H. Despite all of these drawbacks, black families still had two parents in over 80% of their families until the later half of the 20th century when that dropped to under 30%.

Critical Questions

1. How did initial African slave migration begin?

2. How did Saint Augustine figure into black migration patterns?

3. Which areas did blacks migrate to from Saint Augustine?

4. How did black migration proceed after the Civil War?

5. Why was there an increase in the creation of suburbs?

6. Why did successful blacks also want to live in these suburbs?

7. Why did blacks find sailing back to Africa to live permanently an unsatisfying experience?

8. Why has the two-parent black family gradually eroded down to less than 30% over the last 50 years.

Additional Internet Resources for this Lesson
www.loc.gov/exhibits/african/afam008.html
us.history.wisc.edu/hist102/lectures/lecture09.html
scriptorium.lib.duke.edu/slavery/migration.html

LESSON 10 – Midterm Exam and Paper

Areas of Concern:

1. Origins development of African slavery
2. Origins and development of Caribbean slavery
3. Origins and development of Southern Colony slavery
4. Economic and social ramifications of slavery on blacks

LESSON 11 – Free Blacks in American Cities

Chicago Ghetto

Handouts:
Population Maps of Major US Cities circa 1870-1950

Content

A. The first major shift in the population by freed blacks was to both Atlanta and Washington.

B. Poor housing and rampant racism became the norm for blacks moving into major cities.

C. In addition to Washington and Atlanta, blacks steadily began to move into Baltimore, Philadelphia and New York.

D. The railroad was the primary method of migration for blacks after the Civil War.

E. Blacks utilizing the river boats on the Mississippi often migrated to cities such as New Orleans, Saint Louis, Chicago, Cleveland and Detroit.

F. Most blacks did not participate in the gold rushes of the West which brought great population shifts because they were enslaved in all areas of the South. Some free Northern blacks were able to take part in these ventures, but were usually at some type of disadvantage.

G. Other blacks migrated even further north of New York, including Boston, Canada and parts of the upper Midwest.

Critical Questions

1. Why were Atlanta and Washington logical cities for newly freed blacks to migrate?

2. How were living conditions and economic opportunity for blacks compared to whites already living in large cities?

3. Why do you think Baltimore, Philadelphia and New York were cities that many blacks chose to migrate to?

4. How did the recently freed blacks travel?

5. Why did blacks choosing to travel by river eventually choose to live in places like Chicago, Detroit and Saint Louis?

6. Why were blacks not too involved in the gold rushes of 1848, 1858 and the population increases in the West?

7. Why did some blacks migrate even north of New York?

Additional Internet Resources for this Lesson
www.mdcbowen.org/p2/rm/loury.htm
www.bos.frb.org/economic/nerr/rr1997/spring/glsr97_2.htm
college.hmco.com/history/readerscomp/.../ah_010200_blackghettos.htm

LESSON 12 – Blacks and Stereotypes

handouts:
photos of minstrel shows
photos of racist ads running in papers
early films such as "The Jazz Singer"

Content

A. The first stereotype of blacks in the African slave trade was that they were "lazy". Another that quickly followed was that they needed to be whipped in order to do work. Blacks would suffer with the "lazy" label well into the 20th century and are still labeled "lazy" by racists when they are unemployed through no fault of their own.

B. The "lazy" stereotype traveled across the Atlantic to the Caribbean and the Southern colonies. A new stereotype that developed at that time was judging a black man's worth by the shade of his color. If a slave was a lighter shade of brown than other slaves, he or she would be considered to be "better" than darker slaves.

C. The stereotype of shade even penetrated into the black population itself; some blacks would seek out "high yellers" for mating purposes in order to improve their social conditions. Others would intermarry with Hispanic men or women in the hope that their children would less stigmatized.

D. The constant reinforcement that whites were superior to blacks in every facet of life soon took its toll on the psyche of the vast majority of slaves. Self-loathing and condemnation of other blacks were common occurrences.

E. After the Civil War ended and black migration to the cities began, the stereotypes arrived along with the black population. The majority of Northerners were no less racist than the majority of Southerners. The growing spectacle of minstrel shows were the height of insensitivity to blacks.

F. Blacks in the Northern Cities were considered immoral, dirty, lazy, disease-ridden, violent, alcoholics, and thieves. Perfectly respectable black families would move from the South to the North and face these stereotypes on a daily basis. Some of these stereotypes persist to the present day. Minstel perpetuated these stereotypes.

G. Even well into the 20th century in both literature and film, blacks were consistently portrayed as immoral, illiterate, alcoholic, lazy, violent and silly-looking. The first sound film from Hollywood was racist, "The Jazz Singer". Aunt Jemima, Amos and Andy and other black stereotypes also began to appear in various media. Eventually, Hollywood began to seriously consider black entertainers in such films as "Gone With the Wind". Later Sidney Pointier becoming the first major black actor in United States History to escape stereotypical roles in films like "They Call Me Mr. Tibbs" and Lilies of the Field".

Critical Questions

1. How do you think the stereotype of black laziness began?

2. Why was the shade of a black person's skin important?

3. Why would some blacks seek to mate with "high yellers" and Hispanics?

4. Why did some blacks loathe themselves and their black friends?

5. How did blacks find Northerners compared to Southerners in social attitudes?

6. What stereotypes followed blacks into the Northern cities they migrated to?

7. Describe the evolution of blacks in American cinema.

Additional Internet Resources for this Lesson

en.wikipedia.org/wiki/Blackface
www.npr.org/features/feature.php?wfld=1919122
www.tolerance.org/news/article_tol.jsp?id=1054

LESSON 13 – Black Political History

Handouts:
Photos of various black political leaders

Content

    A. The first prominent black political leader was Frederick Douglas, who fought institution of slavery as an abolitionist before the Civil War.

    B. Marcus Garvey's main contribution as a black leader was to redirect the focus from white heroes to black heroes. Blacks, had for too long, been told that all great leaders of the world were white. Marcus Garvey initiated a pride in being black.

C. Some contributions of W.E.B Dubois were: to inaugurate the opening of black officer training schools, began legal proceedings against lynchers of blacks, and set up benefits for returning black veterans.

D. Martin Luther King, probably the most famous of all black political leaders, made tremendous strides in the area of Civil Rights during the later half of the 20th century. He was particularly effective during the 1960s.

E. Malcolm X (also known as Malcolm Little) had a profound effect on the part of the black population who demanded more immediate change in white America's social attitudes towards blacks. Malcolm X was less tolerant of white insensitivity and injustices toward blacks. He was far more strident than Martin Luther King and did not care whether the white community agreed with him or not.

F. Jesse Jackson was the ideological successor to Martin Luther King and tried to build a "rainbow coalition" politically in order to run for the presidency of the United States. He was ultimately unsuccessful in gaining the nomination, but was successful in gaining the recognition of both whites and blacks (as well as the international community) as a force to be reckoned with within the United States political structure.

G. Nelson Mandela was an internationally acclaimed black leader who successfully ended apartheid in South Africa. He went on to be President of South Africa and is recognized the world over as one of the greatest leaders of any movement in the history of politics.

Critical Questions

1. How did Frederick Douglass distinguish himself?
2. How did Marcus Garvey instill pride into the black population?
3. How did W.E.B Dubois advance the plight of blacks?
4. Discuss the accomplishments of Martin Luther King.
5. Why was Malcolm X more radical than Martin Luther King?
6. How was Jesse Jackson able to be so successful politically?
7. Why was Nelson Mandela an important black historical figure?

Additional Internet Resources for this Lesson

www.kn.pacbell.com/wired/BHM/bh_hotlist.html

www.infoplease.com/ipa/A0801534.html

www.blackfacts.com

LESSON 14 – Black Economic Leaders

Handouts:
Photos of Black Economic Leaders

Content

A. George Washington Carver made his fortune through the cultivation of peanuts and through various innovative methods of farming for that product.

B. Barbara Smith was one of the first independently wealthy black women in history who made millions from lifestyle décor design.

C. Willie Gary, a prominent Georgia lawyer listed in Forbes Magazine's top American attorneys, has donated millions to black colleges.

D. Daymund John made millions by targeting black consumers with his clothing line called FUBU (for us, by us). Many major clothing distributors had overlooked this lucrative market and John took advantage of their failings.

E. Tiger Woods crushed a black stereotype as hard as he crushed a golf ball. No longer was the sport of golf the pure dominion of whites. He also made millions through astute marketing skills and advertisements.

F. Bill Cosby has been a life-long educator and has contributed millions to black colleges over the years. He has always stressed the value of education over athletics.

G. Oprah Winfrey is the latest and, by far, the wealthiest of all black entrepreneurs in Black History. She is considered generous to a fault and has given millions to a variety of causes.

Critical Questions

1. Why was it more difficult for George Washington Carver to make his mark than many of the talented blacks who would follow him?

2. Why was the emergence of Barbara Smith so important at the beginning of The 20th century?

3. Why was the mentioning of Willie Gary in Forbes Magazine considered an important advance for blacks?

4. How was Daymond John able to amass his fortune?

5. Why did the emergence of Tiger Woods dissolve a lengthy black stereotype?

6. Why does Bill Cosby believe education is more valuable than athletics?

7. Oprah Winfrey has made far more money than any black athlete in history; what does this say about women and athletics?

Additional Internet Resources for this Lesson
www.stanford.edu/~ccarson/articles/oxford.htm
philanthropy.org/publications/.../african_american_paper.pdf
afgen.com/black_wealth.html

LESSON 15 – Black Religious History

Handouts
Martin Luther King
Elijah Muhammad

Content

A. Phillus Wheatley - Some may argue that this great poet of the latter 18th century was a moralist and not a religious leader, but few would argue that her morality was any lesser than any religious black leader in history.

B. Predating Wheatley by a few hundred years was the Catholic Church influence of the slave-trading countries of Portugal and Spain. Blacks who later became members of this religious group had as much choice to join as they did in becoming slaves. Later-day black Catholics have gradually diminished in number due to the incursion of other religions in the black community.

C. Athough not technically a religious leader, Mahalia Jackson did more for Gospel-singing than anyone in history. This Baptist woman and her music were more beloved than the vast majority of black religious leaders in history.

D. Betsey Stockton, was the slave of a prominent New Jersey educator named Robert Stockton. He gave Betsey to his daughter who was married to a Presbyterian minister. This minister recruited Betsey to be the first black overseas missionary. Presbyterianism, however, went the same way as Catholocism in the black communities with the incursion of influential Baptist and Islamic leaders.

E. Martin Luther King, the second most famous black man in history (Muhammad Ali is the first), was a great religious and political leader of the 50s and 60s. Although a Baptist minister, he was one of the first to forge rainbow coalitions (later copied by Jesse Jackson).

F. Elijah Muhammad – the primary introducer of Islam into the United States community of of religions. Had a running feud with Malcolm X about the direction of Islam in the United States. Muhammad accused of plotting and executing the death of Malcolm X, but that theory was never proven in a court of law.

G. Muhammad Ali – although technically not a religious leader, Ali had greater influence than any other black person in history. His religious beliefs (Islamic) appeared to be more genuine than any religious leader in the United States or the world.

Critical Questons

1. Why was the poetry of Phillus Wheatley so important?

2. Why has Catholicism declined in black communities?

3. How did Mahalia Jackson invigorate the Baptist community?

4. Why has the influence of Betsey Stockton and Presbyterianism declined in the black communities?

5. Why was Martin Luther King so influential?

6. How did Elijah Muhammad change religious options for blacks?

7. Why was Muhammad Ali a great spokesperson for Islam?

Other Internet Resources for this Lesson

religion.**passersbuy.com**/religion/black.**html**
www.uakron.edu/pas/black religion.**html**
www.noi.org

handouts:
Photos and articles on Current Black Leaders

Content

A. The leading consensus black spokesperson entering the 21st Century would
   have to be Jesse Jackson. Jesse Jackson has been a civil rights spokesperson
   since the end of the Martin Luther King era.

B. Another leading spokesperson of the black community in the 21st Century is
   Louis Farrakhan, the current leader of the Nation of Islam. This is the group
   Whose leadership had formerly been contested by both Elijah Muhammad
and Malcolm X. It is often mentioned in editorials that Louis Farrakhan is to Jesse
Jackson as Malcolm X used to be to Martin Luther King.

C. Colin Powell, despite not speaking directly as a partisan leader of blacks, still
   Has respect of millions of black citizens for his performance in the Middle
   East and for his political acumen and connections in Washington DC.

D. Another individual who does not speak directly as a partisan leader of
   blacks, but has the respect of millions within the United States is
   Condoleezza Rice, the current Secretary of State. She is the most powerful
   black woman in the United States.

D. Donna Shalala, the president of Miami University, and one of the first
   advocates of the voucher system of education allowing parents to determine
   which schools their children can attend, is considered by many to be the
   current black educational leader in the United States.

E. Barack Obama, senator from Illinois and advocate for poor and working
   families, has emerged as a new black beacon for this decade.

F. Shape James, the five-term mayor of Newark, has turned Newark around
   from a place that both blacks and whites avoided to a center of black pride.

G. Anthony Williams, the technologically savvy mayor of Washington, DC, has
   made the country forget about the dreadful recent political scandals of that
   city's leadership.

Critical Questions

1. Why is Jesse Jackson still considered the leading black spokesperson of the 21st century?

2. Why would some classify Louis Farrakhan as the natural successor to either Elijah Muhammad or Malcolm X?

3. Why is Colin Powell considered such an important black voice?

4. Why would Donna Shalala be considered one of America's leading educators?

5. Why are some people projecting Barack Obama as a future force to be reckoned with?

6. Why is Sharpe James of Newark considered a politician of substance?

7. Why is Anthony Williams of Washington DC considered a good 21st century leader?

Additional Resources for this Lesson

www.naacp.org
www.cbcpac.com/news/press3.php
search.foxnews.com/info.foxnws/redirs_all.htm?

Lesson 17 – Blacks in Sports

handouts:
Photos of Black Athletes

Content

A. The first black athlete of any note was Jack Johnson, who despite having the cards stacked against him, became the heavyweight champion of the world at the turn of the 20th century.

B. Other great boxers included Joe Louis and Muhammad Ali who both influenced millions.

C. In baseball, Hank Aaron was a source of black pride as he broke Babe Ruth's home run record of 714.

D. In football Jim Brown became the first great black running back with national exposure.

E. In basketball, Micheal Jordan has already become a legend in American sports.

G. Tiger Woods has ended the stereotype that blacks could not compete in golf and Althea Gibson did the same for black women in the sport of tennis. Arthur Ashe was the first black man to break that barrier in tennis.

H. In baseball, Jackie Robinson and Larry Doby broke the race barrier in the late 1940s. Satchel Paige had labored away in the Negro leagues for over a decade before he could bring his talents to the majors in the late 1940s.

Critical Questions

1. Why was boxing a popular choice for black athletes?

2. How did Joe Louis and Muhammad Ali influence their fans?

3. Why were Hank Aaron's accomplishments so important?

4. Why do you think basketball is the number one choice of most young black athletes?

5. Why did Micheal Jordan become the undisputed greatest basketball idol in the history of the black community?

6. How did Tiger Woods have an important impact on the black community?

7. Why were Althea Gibson and Arthur Ashe's breakthrough efforts in tennis

important?

8. Why were Jackie Robinson and Larry Doby's breakthrough efforts in baseball important?

Additional Internet Resources for this Lesson
www.time.com/time/time100/heroes/profile/robinson01.html
www.lib.berkeley.edu/MRC/AfricanAmVid.html
en.wikipedia.org/wiki/Jack_Johnson

LESSON 18 – Black Educational Leaders

handouts:

Photos and Stories of Black Educational Leaders

Content

A. The first significant black educational leader was Booker T. Washington, attended what is now Hampton University and went on to found Tuskegee University, a leading trainer of black teachers.

B. George Washington Carver was a direct recruit of Booker T. Washington. He became active at Tuskegee as a trainer of black farmers and teachers.

C. Frederick Douglas Patterson was a great force in black education because he founded the United Negro College Fund which allowed Many qualified blacks to become teachers.

D. Charles L. Reason was a triple-threat educator. He was also a fervent abolitionist before the Civil War and a widely read poet. His poetry often had slavery as its focal point.

E. Emmett Scott became the successor to Booker T Washington and the progress at Tuskegee Institute.

F. Edward Franklin Frazier earned his PHD from Chicago University in 1931 during the depths of the Depression. He went on to teach over 20 years at Howard University.

G. Harriet Beecher Stowe, although not technically an educator, educated the American public to the horrors of slavery through her book, *Uncle Tom's Cabin.*

Critical Questions

1. Why is Booker T. Washington considered the greatest black educator of all time?

2. How did George Washington Carver educate blacks in two different ways?

3. Why was Frederick Douglas Patterson vital to so many black Students?

4. How many ways did Charles L. Reason attack slavery?

5. How did Emmett Scott contribute to black education?

6. Why was education a difficult road for Edward Franklin Frazier?

7. Why was Harriet Beecher Stowe one of the most influential of all educators?

Additional Internet Resources for this Lesson
www.nabse.org
www.cabse.org
www.h-net.org/reviews/showrev.cgi?path

Lesson 19 – Notable Black Contributions

handouts:

Photos and Stories of Great Black Contributions

Content

A. Marcus Garvey – started a black nationalist movement to take blacks back to Africa.

B. Harriet Tubman – operated the Underground Railroad before the the Emancipation Proclamation.

C. Whitney Young Jr. – director and proactive leader of the Urban League.

D. Dred Scott – slave who sued for his freedom and lost because the United States Supreme Court ruled against him.

E. Nat Turner – slave who physically revolted against slavery in Virginia during an 1831 uprising.

F. Bessie Smith – blues singer icon who was responsible for the art form spreading across the United States.

H. Nat King Cole – mainstream singer who was the first black man to successfully penetrate the mass market in record sales. Later followed by his daughter, Natalie.

I. Spike Lee – movie director with many black themes running through his films. Films proved to be financial successes with mainstream audiences, also.

Critical Questions

1. Why was the Marcus Garvey movement important?

2. Why were Harriet Tubman's activities extremely dangerous?

3. How did Whitney Young Jr. contribute to the black movement?

4. Why was the Dred Scott Decision of the Supreme Court a stain on the

history of America?

5. Why was Nat Turner doomed to failure?

6. How did Bessie Smith influence blacks in America?

7. Why was Nat King Cole significant to the entertainment field?

8. Why is Spike Lee so important to black culture?

Additional Internet Resources for this Lesson
www.elboricua.com/AfroBorinquen_people.html
www.askart.com/interest/blackamerican_a.asp
worldcatlibraries.org

Lesson 20 – Final Exam/Paper

Rosa Parks being fingerprinted for Civil Disobedience

Areas of Concern

1. Black role models
2. Black political action
3. Black economic initiatives

Using the three variables above, create a model using at least two of them to push forward an issue is that is in need of change within the black community. Be thorough with your business or political action plan. Be sure to consider many of the objections and obstacles that will be placed in your path.

www.ingramcontent.com/pod-product-compliance
Lightning Source LLC
Chambersburg PA
CBHW070130290526
45789CB00005B/2190